Greetings from RADIATOR SPRINGS

GATEWAY TO THE ORNAMENT VALLEY

Disney · PIXAR

Cars

Illustrated by the Disney Storybook Artists, Marianne Tucker, and Andy Phillipson
Inspired by the character designs created by Pixar Animation Studios

Walter Foster

W9-DDI-915

2
6117433147

226 0881

J
741.51

L

Managing Editor: Rebecca J. Razo
Art Director: Shelley Baugh
Production Artist: Debbie Aiken

Materials and characters from the movies Cars and Cars 2. Copyright © 2011 Disney/Pixar.

Disney/Pixar elements © Disney/Pixar, not including underlying vehicles owned by third parties; and, if applicable: Hudson Hornet, Pacer, and Gremlin are trademarks of Chrysler LLC; Porsche is a trademark of Porsche; FIAT is a trademark of FIAT S.p.A.

No license is herein granted for the use of any drawing of a Disney character for any commercial purpose, including, but not limited to, the placing of any such drawing on an article of merchandise or the reproduction, public display, or sale of any such drawing. Any use other than home use by the reader of any such drawing is prohibited.

Table of Contents

Disney · PIXAR

Cars

It's time for the biggest race of the year, the Dinoco 400. In this world, cars are the characters, and rookie Lightning McQueen rolls out of his trailer to swarming reporters and cheering fans.

The winner of the race will get the coveted Piston Cup trophy. The three top contenders are seven-time Piston Cup winner The King, perennial runner-up Chick Hicks, and new hotshot Lightning McQueen. And with The King retiring, his lucrative Dinoco sponsorship is also up for grabs.

Lightning takes the lead! But at his pit stop, he refuses to change tires to save time. In the final lap, his rear tires blow! Chick and The King catch up. The race is too close to call!

While they wait for the results, Lightning is daydreaming about his future glory . . . until he learns the race was a three-way tie! A tie-breaker race will be held in California in one week.

Reluctantly Lightning makes a quick appearance for Rust-eze, his current sponsor. Then he backs into his trailer and hits the road with his driver, Mack. After many long hours, Mack dozes off. He swerves and Lightning falls out of the trailer!

Lost and panicked, Lightning speeds through the small town of Radiator Springs. The Sheriff takes chase, making backfire noises that cause Lightning to drive wildly, tearing up the asphalt street.

The next morning, Lightning wakes up in the town impound. The Sheriff orders the friendly, rusty tow truck named Mater to tow Lightning to traffic court.

In court, Sally, the town's attorney, argues that the ruined road will turn away desperately needed customers. Doc, the judge, sentences Lightning to stay until he fixes the road.

Lightning is hooked to the messy paver named Bessie. After an hour he says he's finished, but the road looks terrible. Doc challenges Lightning to a race. If Lightning wins, he can go. But if Lightning loses, he will have to stay and finish the road Doc's way.

When the race begins, Lightning leaves Doc in the dust but ends up running into a cactus patch.

That night, Lightning goes back to work. By morning, there is a newly paved street. The townsfolk are inspired, so they begin fixing up their shops.

Later, Sally overhears Lightning explaining that winning the Piston Cup means he'll have fame, fortune, and a big new sponsor. He even promises Mater a helicopter ride!

The next morning Lightning wanders into Doc's office, where he finds three Piston Cups and realizes that Doc is the fabulous Hudson Hornet! Doc shoos away Lightning.

Later, Lightning secretly watches Doc racing at the dirt track. Doc finally lets out his secret: When he returned to the racing world after recovering from a big wreck, Doc was replaced by a rookie just like Lightning.

The next morning, Mater awakens the town to show them that the road is finished. Then Lightning goes shopping, and he becomes the best customer Radiator Springs has seen in a long time.

But the mood is crushed by an invasion of reporters. Lightning has been found. Mack takes him to the big race. Lightning tries to prepare, but his heart isn't in it.

As the race begins, Lightning falls far behind . . . until he sees his pals from Radiator Springs have come to be his pit crew!

When Chick causes The King to crash behind him, Lightning hears the crowd's reaction and looks up at the stadium screen. He thinks of Doc's crash. Lightning slams on the breaks just before the finish line.

Chick wins the race, but no one cares. Lightning reverses and pushes The King to a second-place finish. The crowd goes wild!

Lightning is offered the Dinoco sponsorship! But he decides to stay with the loyal guys from Rust-eze. He does ask Dinoco for one favor though: a helicopter ride for his friend Mater.

Alone on the mountain, Sally looks out over the valley when Lightning tells her he's opening up his headquarters in town. Their moment is interrupted as Mater appears in the helicopter, singing. Sally laughs and tears off down the mountain. Lightning chases her. There's nowhere else he'd rather be.

Disney · PIXAR

Cars 2

Finn McMissile, a slick car on a secret mission, is spying on a criminal named Professor Z on an oil derrick in the middle of the Pacific ocean. He's about to uncover a convoluted plot when he's spotted by Gremlins and Pacers—the "Lemons." They chase Finn and destroy him—or so they think. Finn escapes unharmed.

Back in Radiator Springs, Lightning McQueen is fresh off his win at the Hudson Hornet Memorial Piston Cup Race. During dinner, Lightning's attention turns to the T.V. Italian race car Francesco Bernoulli is taunting Lightning, daring him to compete in the World Grand Prix sponsored by Miles Axlerod and his alternative fuel Allinol. Lightning rises to the challenge, and "Team Lightning McQueen" heads to Tokyo for the first leg of the race.

In Tokyo at a fancy World Grand Prix party, Finn McMissile and fellow British Agent Holley Shiftwell are undercover, waiting to receive a top-secret device from American Agent Rod "Torque" Redline.

In Mater's excitement at the party, he appears to leak oil in front of Miles Axlerod—much to Lightning's horror. Lightning tells Mater he is embarrassing him and sends Mater to the bathroom to clean up. While Mater is inside a stall, two Lemons corner Torque in the bathroom. As Mater exits, Torque plants the device on him—but Mater doesn't know. Holley detects the device and mistakes Mater for the American spy. She arranges a meeting with him, but Mater thinks they have a date!

Professor Z realizes that the device has been passed to Mater. He instructs his minions, Grem and Acer, to find the tow truck. On race day, the cars fill up with Allinol and hit the track. During the race, Grem and Acer aim Professor Z's special "camera" at an unsuspecting race car. The camera beam causes the Allinol to boil—and explode! Later, Axlerod defends Allinol and reassures the public that his fuel is completely safe.

Holley speaks to Mater on his headset and guides him out of the pit for his safety. Mater repeats Holley's instructions out loud, but Lightning thinks Mater is directing him on the racetrack. He follows Mater's "racing tips" and loses to Francesco. Lightning blames Mater. Saddened, Mater decides to head home.

At the airport, Holley and Finn intercept Mater. Holley locates and opens the device to reveal a photograph of an old, gas-guzzling engine that they are not able to identify. Finn suggests visiting Tomber in Paris. If anyone can identify an engine, it's Tomber. The trio heads to Paris, but Tomber can't identify the engine. Mater tells them that the engine belongs to a Lemon. Tomber tells them that the four Lemon families have planned a Lemonhead meeting in Porto Corsa, Italy—where the second leg of the race will be. Finn, Holley, and Mater head to Italy hoping to get more information.

In Italy, Lightning meets Luigi's Uncle Topolino and tells him about the fight with Mater. Topolino reminds Lightning that best friends may fight, but it's always important to make up fast. Lightning is filled with regret.

Meanwhile, Holley disguises Mater as a Lemon's tow truck and equips him with voice-activated spy gadgets. Mater sneaks into the meeting while Holley and Finn listen in. Someone is trying to make Allinol appear dangerous so that everyone will go back to using gasoline! Later, at the race, Grem and Acer blow up several more race cars with the camera.

At the meeting, Mater overhears Professor Z order the Lemons to kill Lightning. Mater tries to leave to warn Lightning, but the Lemons capture him and reveal that a bomb is planted in Lightning's pit. Mater breaks free and rushes off to find Lightning. But he soon realizes the bomb is attached to him. Only the voice of the one who activated it can deactivate it!

Lightning and Mater are reunited, but Mater tries to keep away from Lightning. He doesn't want his friend to get hurt if the bomb goes off. Lightning refuses to leave Mater. He wants to apologize.

Finn captures Professor Z, and Holley takes care of the Lemon goons. Finally, Mater understands who is behind the plot to destroy the race cars and defame Allinol. Mater hooks onto Lightning and deploys his rocket thrusters and parachute. Mater and Lightning fly over London and land at Buckingham Palace—right before the Queen! With a minute to spare, Mater explains that someone is sabotaging

the race. "It's him!" Mater says, pointing at Axlerod. Mater explains that the secret oil derricks belong to Axlerod, who invented Allinol to make alternative fuel look bad so cars would have to keep using the gasoline made from his oil!

With the bomb timer still ticking, Axlerod says, "Deactivate." The bomb stops—proving his guilt. His intention was to make all Lemons wealthy and powerful because they have lived in the shadows all their lives, being treated as second-rate cars. He wanted the Lemons to get the respect they've waited so long for. Mater is knighted by the Queen for uncovering the plot.

The gang heads back to Radiator Springs with all the race cars to finish the final leg of the race. Finn and Holley come too—they have a new assignment for Mater! But Mater politely declines.

He is just fine where he is.

Getting Started

Ready, set, go! That's right, you're off and ready to draw, color, and paint your way to creating revved-up cars. Though Lightning McQueen may require some fancy tools for a tune-up, all you need are a few simple supplies to draw this race car and all his pals. A graphite pencil will get your drawing engine running. Then you can spice up things by moving on to color with felt-tip markers, colored pencils, watercolors, or acrylic paints. Be sure to use the tips in this book to keep these cars in prime condition. Ready to roll? *Ka-chow!*

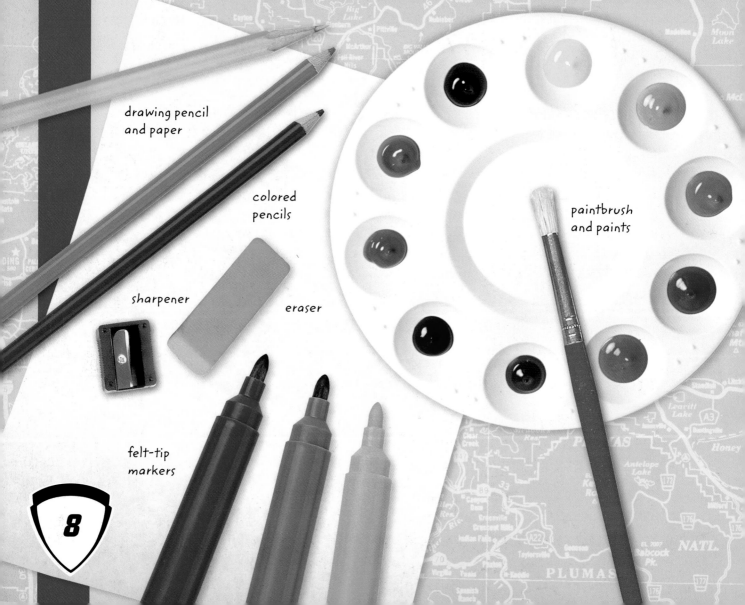

drawing pencil and paper

colored pencils

paintbrush and paints

sharpener

eraser

felt-tip markers

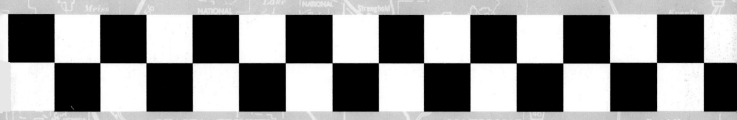

Just follow the simple steps!

Step 1

First draw the basic shapes.

Step 2

Each new step is shown in blue.

Step 3

Simply follow the blue lines to add the details.

Step 4

Now darken the lines you want to keep and erase the rest.

Use crayons, markers, colored pencils, or paints to add color to your drawing.

9

Lightning McQueen

Lightning McQueen is a worldwide celebrity whose every dream has come true. Famous, successful, and surrounded by great friends, Lightning is ready to enjoy time in the slow lane—just as soon as he wins the World Grand Prix.

Step 1

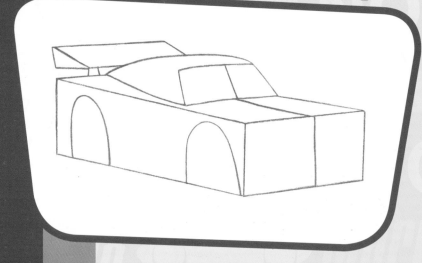

while he's competing in the races of the World Grand Prix, Lightning sports this tribute to Doc Hudson on his hood.

Step 2

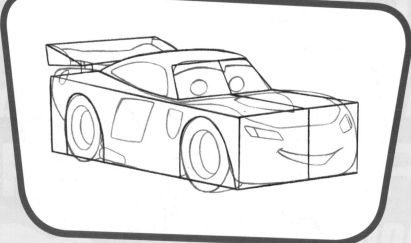

Step 3

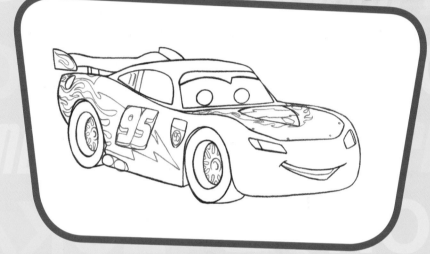

for the WGP races, Lightning gets a new, sportier spoiler!

Step 4

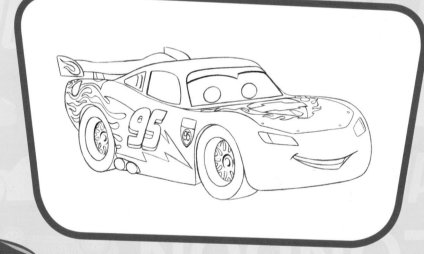

11

Mater

Mater is a friendly tow truck with a big heart, who is always willing to lend a helping hook. He is the self-proclaimed world's best backward driver. In Cars 2, Mater gets caught up in a world of espionage when he accompanies Lightning to the World Grand Prix.

Step 1

YES!
mirrors are at irregular angles

NO!
mirrors are not perfectly aligned

Step 2

THE OIL PAN

keep facial expressions off center to emphasize Mater's goofiness

YES!

YES!

NO!
too centered

Step 4

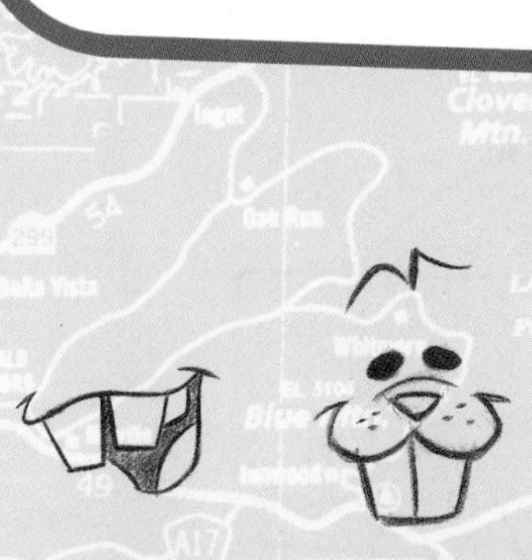

YES!

NO!

his misshapen buckteeth aren't perfect squares—and there's a gap between them

13

Sally

In Cars, Sally, a smart and beautiful sports car, is determined to restore Radiator Springs to the bustling town it was in its heyday. Originally an attorney from Los Angeles, she shows Lightning that sometimes it's good to live life in the slow lane. In Cars 2, Sally shows Lightning her support by showing up for the final leg of the World Grand Prix.

Step 1

Sally's eyebrows are heaviest at the peaks

YES!

NO!

Step 2

Step 3

Sally is just about a tire width smaller than Lightning

Step 4

YES!
spokes
have
curved
pattern

NO!
not
straight

NO!
not
sharp

15

Luigi and Guido

Luigi is an Italian sports car who runs Casa Della Tires in Radiator Springs. Guido is an Italian forklift. In Cars 2, they volunteer to be in Lightning's pit crew at the World Grand Prix. They're thrilled that the second race in Porto Corsa, Italy is located near their hometown!

Step 1

Step 2

NO!

not hard edges

YES!

edges are rounded

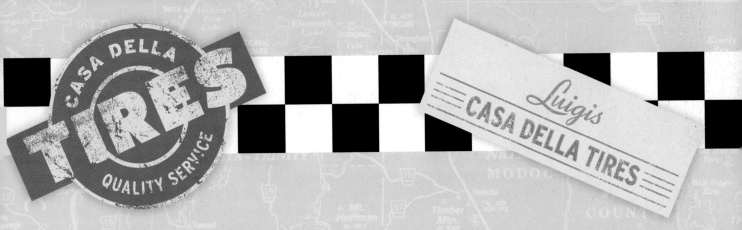

Step 1

Step 2

YES! head is wider at base

NO! head is not square

Finn McMissile

British Agent Finn McMissile is sleek, charming, intelligent, and loaded with cool gadgets! Finn knows there's a conspiracy afoot at the World Grand Prix. With the help of fellow British Agent Holley Shiftwell—and Mater—he and his colleagues are destined to uncover the plot.

Step 1

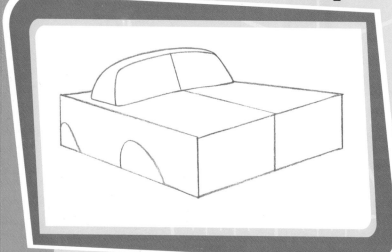

Finn has a built-in missile launcher and can fire grappling hooks

Step 2

when his pupils are slightly covered by his eyelids, it conveys how cool he looks

Step 3

Finn can transform into a hydroplane

he has large top teeth, which should be the predominant feature in his mouth

Step 4

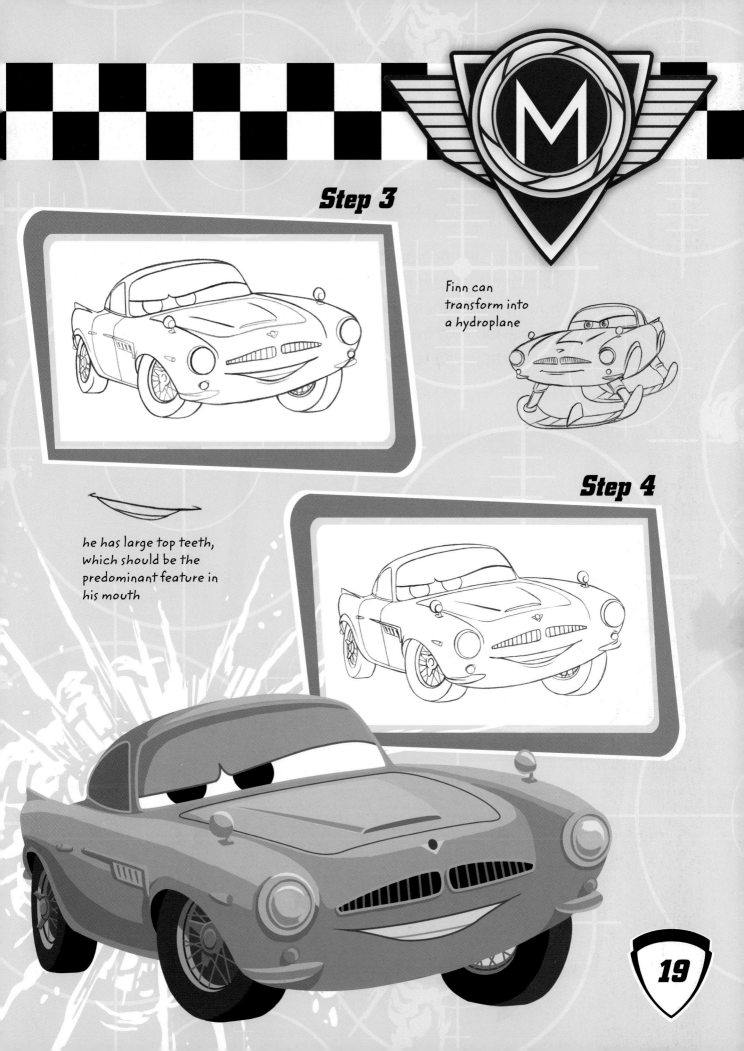

Holley Shiftwell

Beautiful, young agent-in-training Holley Shiftwell knows all the standard operating procedures of top-secret work—and she knows how to follow them! Fresh out of the Academy, Holley gets her on-the-job field training by working to solve the World Grand Prix conspiracy with veteran Agent Finn McMissile.

Step 1

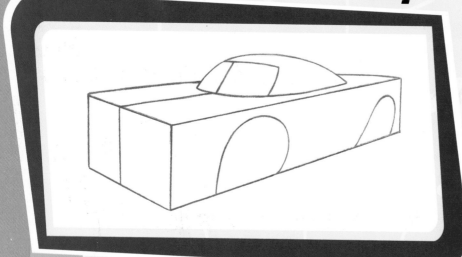

Holley has secret weapons, such as wings

Step 2

from the side, Holley can be constructed from smooth interlocking shapes with almost no sharp angles

Holley has full lips

NO!
too simple

NO!
too thin

YES!

Holley has a screen that projects from her front turn indicators

Francesco Bernoulli

International racing champ Francesco Bernoulli loves a good, clean race—almost as much as he adores himself. Francesco challenges Lightning McQueen to participate in the World Grand Prix. He even wins the first leg! Arrivederci!

Step 1

Francesco's "head" works like a helmet sitting down into the body with the air intake above

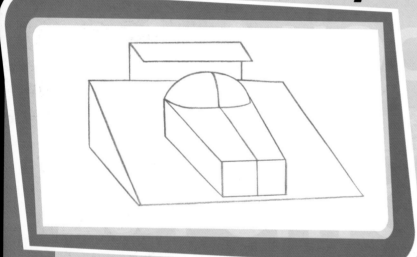

Step 2

YES!

NO!

because his mouth is so far away from his eyes, his expressions will read more easily when he's turned more toward us rather than to the side

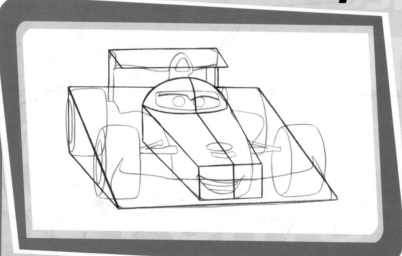

Step 3

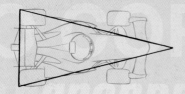

his basic body shape is a wedge that slices through the air for maximum speed!

Step 4

Francesco sits lower to the ground than Lightning

23

Professor Z

The smart and savvy mad scientist Professor Z has mastered the art of sophisticated weapons design and has created an elaborate device disguised as a camera that can harm cars without leaving a trace of evidence. His goal is to sabotage the World Grand Prix racers. Will he succeed?

Step 1

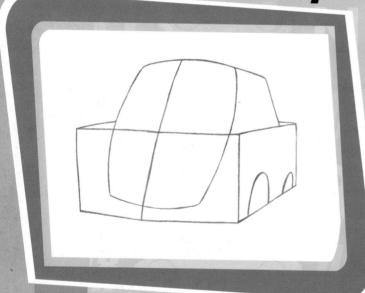

Professor Z is really small

Professor Z looks the same coming or going!

Step 2

his broken roof rack gives the appearance of a hair comb-over

WGP

Step 3

be careful when posing Professor Z that his body angle doesn't cause his eye to be cut across by his monocle

YES!

NO!

Step 4

25

Acer

Acer is one of Professor Z's main goons who carries out all of his dirty work. This Lemon, along with his buddy Grem, enjoys taking out the World Grand Prix racers one by one by aiming the TV camera device at them while they're zooming down the racetrack.

Step 1

Acer has a very tall cab; don't make it too short

NO!

YES!

Step 2

keep body shape simple, boxy, and soft

Step 3

Grem and Acer are
roughly the same size

Step 4

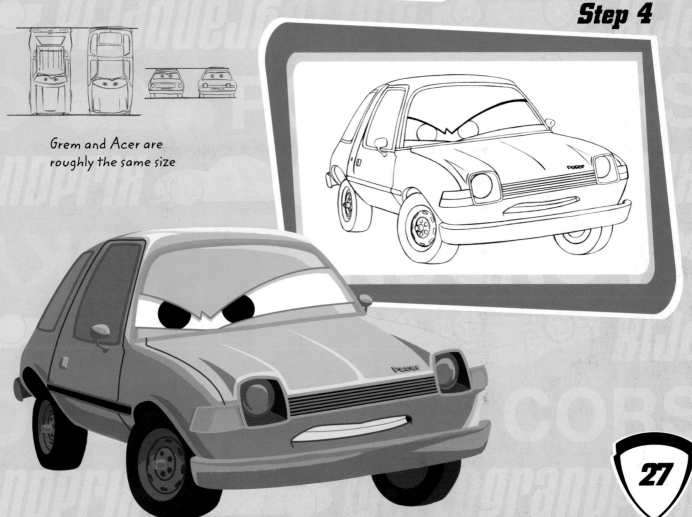

Grem

Grem is another of Professor Z's goons. Grem and his partner-in-crime, Acer, don't have the fancy gadgets that the spy cars have. But they are tough and relentless. They'll do anything to stop the secret agents!

Step 1

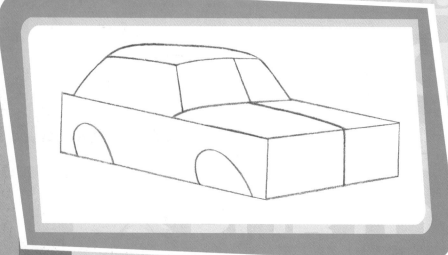

Grem has a distinctive decal on his side that resembles a hockey stick

Step 2

draw lower eyelids to make his expressions more shifty

from behind, his body shape looks like an upside-down cup on a saucer

Step 3

his front grille looks like a moustache, and he's missing some teeth because he's been in some fights

Step 4

when they're doing their dirty work, Grem and Acer are in contact with their boss by wearing headsets

29

Miles Axlerod

Sir Miles Axlerod has devoted his life and fortune—acquired as an oil baron—to creating a renewable, alternative fuel called Allinol, which he showcases at a three-country race called the World Grand Prix. But Mater and his friends soon discover that Allinol isn't all it's cracked up to be—and neither is Axlerod.

Step 1

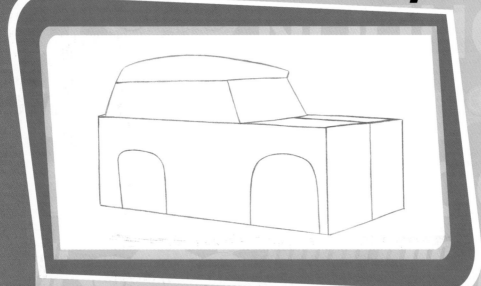

he has a very boxy appearance from the front

Step 2

30

Step 3

a winch on the back
carries his electrical plug

Step 4

the top of his cab
should resemble an
English driving cap

31

Siddeley

Whenever Finn McMissile is in a tight situation, Siddeley is there to bail him out! This super sleek British spy plane is equipped with weapons, gadgetry, computers, surveillance equipment, and much more. Siddeley is a top-notch spy who always travels in style.

Step 1

Step 2

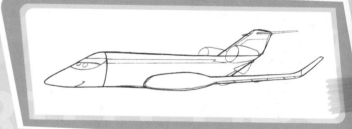

Step 3

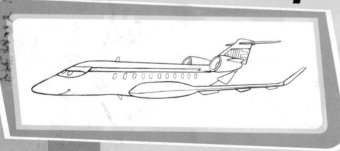

Step 4

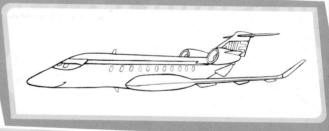